Illuminations

Bruce Kaduk

Morning Star Books
Post Office Box 50533
Palo Alto, California 94303

Second Edition

PUBLISHED BY MORNING STAR BOOKS
Palo Alto, California 94303

Library of Congress Catalog Card Number: 92-91160
ISBN 0-9621914-7-7

Printed in the United States of America

For my mother and father

All the opposing qualities
that are in nature—
order and disorder
tranquility and fury
chance and design
diversity and uniformity—
are in man as well.
The contradictions of man
reflect the
contradictions of nature.

The mind that questions and explores
can be nothing other
than passionate
in its outlook.

The most profound aspects
of life
have a simplicity
about them.
It is no surprise
that some of the greatest minds
have probed the most elementary particles.

Deluged by passionate desires,
barraged by irrational fears,
rampaged by incessant wanting,
our souls are sculpted
by the violent precipitation
of privately experienced storms.

Out of neurons and synapses
out of fibers and impulses
out of sensory cells and motor cells
out of cerebra and cerebella
has arisen,
like a newly created star
illuminating an otherwise
unknown universe,
the phenomenon
of human intelligence.

The degree to which we are happy
is proportional
to the amount of harmony that exists
between
what we do and
what we are, by nature, inclined to do.

From the point of view
of human observation
the world is a combination
of five billion perspectives.

What is it
that governs the operation
of your heart
and your brain
and your muscles,
if it is not the same thing
that governs the operation
of the planets
and the stars
and the galaxies?

Go ask any dancer why he chose the work that he chose
  and he'll tell you
  it's the rhythm of the sound
  and the beat
  and he'll tell you
  the rhythm is in his blood.
Go ask any astronomer why he chose the work that he chose
  and he'll tell you
  it's the rhythm of the earth
  and the moon
  and he'll tell you
  the rhythm is in his blood.
Go ask any historian why he chose the work that he chose
  and he'll tell you
  it's the rhythm of the rise
  and the fall,
  the creating and the destroying
  and he'll tell you
  the rhythm is in his blood.
Go ask any man why he'd choose life over death
  and he'll tell you
  it's the rhythm
  it's the rhythm
  it's the rhythm
  and he'll tell you
  the rhythm is in his blood.

Not by means of
  the most sophisticated computer
  the most subtle instrument
  the most elaborate apparatus
Not by means of anything
  except the human mind—
can beauty be perceived.

Don't believe anybody who tells you
about simple answers and easy solutions.
We think of Einstein
as the guy who had all the answers.
He spent the last twenty years of his life
on a problem
he never did solve.

A magnificent form
moving gracefully
and energetically
through space,
man is nothing
without
arms embracing
legs stretching
bodies twisting
eyes dancing
lips kissing
hands touching
faces expressing
minds reaching.

We are standing
in the midst
of events which are changing and
in the midst
of laws which are permanent.

You were not put
on this planet,
    the existence of which
    is still a mystery and
    the size of which is inconsequential
    in comparison to the size of the universe,
in order to be dominated
by the opinions
of other people.

Einstein's equations are not
intellectual exercises.
They are explanations of phenomena
that are occurring,
at this moment,
in the world that each of us
is perceiving.

In the tiniest atom
there is a universe of logic.

It is only emotion
that can transform the soul.
It is love or
    pain or
    yearning or
    pleasure—
It is only emotion
that can transform the soul
and transport it,
for an hour or
for a lifetime,
to a higher level
of existence.

The mere attempt
to do something imaginative
is itself
a liberation.

The artist
is the person
who persists
in exploring
those places within himself
that everyone else
long ago
abandoned.

Governed, on the outside,
by the dictates of
    fortune and
    circumstance and
    time—
governed, on the inside,
by the dictates of
    passion and
    desire and
    fear—
nevertheless,
man still believes in the idea
and in the possibility
of freedom.

You can be absolutely sure
not that your greatest wish
will be fulfilled,
but that if it is,
it will be replaced
by another.

When fearful thoughts
enter our minds,
other thoughts
are thereby excluded.
The latter,
as much as the former,
is the tragedy of fear.

No one knows yet
all there is to know
about the chemistry and physics
of even one drop of water.

It is better
that
the question be left
unanswered
than
the answer be left
unquestioned.

Composed of matter
we can yet understand the nature of matter.
Existing in space
we can yet form conceptions of space.
Living in time
we can yet imagine the infinity of time.

One idea
is the synthesis
of a million
sensations.

We must become conscious
of the beauty that exists
and begin to breathe it
and touch it.
Our best guarantee
for finding happiness in the future
is to find it
at this moment.

Every fact we know
reflects a larger principle.
Every form we observe
reflects a larger order.
Every idea we understand
reflects a larger truth.

Unlike material objects,
love has neither height
nor width.
All it has is depth.

If tomorrow
a new universal law
is discovered,
it will be new only for us.
With respect to
the scheme of nature,
it has existed
from the very beginning.

Once you find that part
within you
that is extraordinary,
and do not doubt
that it is there,
you will find it
in everything else
that exists.

Every human being
is placed
in his own
particular
predicament.

Always look
at the other side
at the other perspective
at the other idea
at the other opinion
because
that which is real and
that which is true
is a combination and
a synthesis.

Endowed
with a body that can perceive what is real and
with a mind that can conceive what is ideal,
why should it be a surprise
that man is in conflict
with himself?

No one—
    not the philosopher
    not the scientist
    not the theologian—
understands the causes of everything.
And so, each of us,
to one degree or another,
lives under an illusion.

Creativity
is a communion
with
the deepest and
most authentic
parts
of ourselves.

It is the questions that will live on.
Long after the debates on whether
    the soul is immortal
    the universe is immortal
    pure thought is immortal
    anything at all is immortal
have quieted down,
it is the questions that will live on,
it is the questions that will remain,
it is the questions that will achieve
    true immortality.

Emotional responses can be understood
and sometimes they can be controlled,
but they cannot
be extinguished.

We plan and
we plan and
we plan
but everything
still turns out to be
an astonishment.

Mountains soaring,
volcanoes erupting,
rivers surging,
winds raging,
fires smoldering,
oceans undulating—
the earth,
not unlike the creatures
who inhabit it,
has urges
and longings
of its own.

As to whether man has intelligence,
there is no question.
As to what end that intelligence will be directed,
there is no other question.

For all of nature's power and force,
it has no consciousness.
Nature acts,
but for no reason of which it is aware.
For all of man's fragility
in relation to the forces of nature,
man has a consciousness.
Man has the ability to act
for a reason.

It is likely that there are
laws of human nature
as universal and eternal
as the laws which govern
atoms and molecules and
planets and galaxies.
That these laws of human nature
are not yet clearly defined
may be due to the fact
that there are no impartial observers.

In every pain and
in every anguish and
in every predicament
lie the seeds
for the birth
of spiritual courage.

The most important element
of intelligence
is the ability
to see another person
or a situation
from more than
one's own particular perspective.

Somewhere around one million
or ten million
or a hundred million
interconnections of nerve impulses
is all it takes
to perceive
the beauty
of one sunset.

Each of us is drawn
to the people and the places and the ideas
we love
by forces
which are as universal
as those responsible for the attraction
of one object to another
by the forces of gravity
and the forces of magnetism.

The woods
the skies
the oceans—
are imbued
with perfection.

To the extent that
a person responds to
    the beauty
    the mystery
    the harmony
of nature,
to that extent
he has become part of
something that has always been,
something that will always be,
something that is eternal and timeless.

Our illusions and
our misconceptions
lack nothing
except accuracy.

There is no pleasure we have felt,
there is no desire we have known,
there is no pain we have suffered—
that has not made its imprint on our minds.

Each new thing that you try is an experiment.
It is not a question of success or failure.
If the experiment fails, you haven't failed.
You have found out something new,
about yourself.

Nothing in the universe
is more real
than what you feel
in your heart.

Within every human being
lies unknown territory
waiting to be discovered.

About the Author

Bruce Kaduk was born and raised in Easton, Pennsylvania. After graduating from Franklin and Marshall College, he attended Rutgers University where he received a Ph.D. degree in chemistry. An industrial scientist, he is the co-author of several technical articles and patents. He resides in Mountain View, California.